RhymAmusings

RhymAmusings

AmuseRimes by **Pierre Coran**

Translated by
Norman R. Shapiro

BWP wishes to thank Librairie Générale Française for allowing us to present this bilingual edition of *AmuseRimes* by Pierre Coran. All the poems within this book are © Livre de Poche Jeunesse, 2015. English language translations © Norman R. Shapiro, 2019. Black Widow Press edition © 2019. All rights reserved.

Black Widow Press is an imprint of Commonwealth Books, Inc., Boston, MA. Distributed to the trade by NBN (National Book Network) throughout North America, Canada, and the U.K. All Black Widow Press books are printed on acid-free paper, and glued into bindings. Black Widow Press and its logo are registered trademarks of Commonwealth Books, Inc.

Publication of this book has also been aided by a grant from the Thomas and Catharine McMahon Fund of Wesleyan University, established through the generosity of the late Joseph McMahon.

Joseph S. Phillips and Susan J. Wood, Ph.D., Publishers

www.blackwidowpress.com

Illustrations: Thomas Baas
Book production: Kerrie L. Kemperman
Cover design: Kerrie L. Kemperman

ISBN-13: 978-0-9995803-5-6

Printed in the United States

10 9 8 7 6 5 4 3 2 1

Pour Irène, Else et Carl,
ma famille en poésie

Qui se nourrit de poésie
peut se permettre d'être
gourmand.

For Dimitri,
with smiles long remembered...
Uncles Norm and Sean

Table of Contents

Preface

Readers of my previous translations of Pierre Coran—
Fables in a Modern Key (2014) and *Fables of Town
and Country* (2017)—will, I imagine, have a good idea
what to expect from the present collection.

RhymAmusings... These seventy-eight delightful
rhyme-vignettes, mini-fables in their own right, will
remind them that Coran (pseud. Eugène Delaisse),
while enjoying a happy reputation in his native Bel-
gium and beyond as a pre-eminent children's poet
and novelist, speaks rather with an adult sophistica-
tion and endearing grace to "the child in all of us."
Typical of the numerous award-winning volumes
hallmarked by his whimsy and wit, and abetted here,
by Thomas Baas's vigorously appropriate illustrations,
these *AmuseRimes* will help explain why Pierre Coran
is a national—and international—treasure.

I trust they will also leave the Anglophone reader
hoping for more...

Norman R. Shapiro

Pour faire un poème

Pour faire un poème,
Tu fermes les yeux

Et en toi, presque aussitôt
Comme sortis d'un chapeau,

Des images naissent,
Des mots apparaissent

Que ta bouche dit,
Que ta main écrit
Dès les yeux rouverts.

Tu relis les vers
De ta poésie,
Les revois un peu

Puis tu les copies
Sur un papier bleu.

To Write a Poem

To write a poem, you
Must do what poets do.

First shut your eyes. And, just like that,
In nothing flat,

Like rabbit from a hat, you pull
A top-hatful—

Words, images, born by the score—
And out they pour...

Eyes open, then, your mouth recites them
And your hand writes them.

Rehash, rehearse
Each line of verse,
Re-read each one...

When all is said and done,
You take a velum sheet,
And copy down your poem, nice and neat...

Imaginaire

Dans *imaginaire*,
Que de mots cachés :

gamin, gamine,
marin, marine,

mage et *mirage,*
rime et *image,*

air et *aire,*
main et *mer,*

gain et *gaine,*
grain et *graine.*

— Assez, assez !
J'ai la *migraine.*

Imagine and Imaginary *

Two words: *imagine* and *imaginary*...
How many other words hiding therein!

Image, air, airy,
Gain, grain, and gin,

Gym, game, grime, grin,
Grim, mirage, genii, magi, age,

Manage and *manager* and *rage,*
Yam, gram, gamine,

Mare and *marine,*
Men, man, and *many,*

Enigma, any,
Rain, reign, regain, remain...
Migraine!

Enough! Enough, for goodness' sake,
Before you make my poor head ache!

Again... Again?... No, not again!
No more! *Amen!*

---

* The poet agrees with my decision to use two related words to his one, thereby spawning more—and more striking and varied—words than a single one could generate.

L' aspic

Quand un aspic
Pique un Aztèque,
Tout le Mexique
Va aux obsèques.

Et quand l'aspic
N'ennuie personne ?

Les Mexicains,
Tout aussitôt,
Piquent un somme
Sous leur chapeau.

The Asp

When an asp bites an Aztec, all
Mexico joins the wake, the funeral,
For his poor, fang-envenomed sake.

But when
The asp plays tame, draws back his arrow—
Head darting, forked tongue taut? What then?

All Mexico, haunch-hunched, posing like sphinx,
Grabs forty winks,
Dozing beneath its broad sombrero.

Parapluie parasol

Au pays des parapluies
S'en alla un parasol.

Au pays des parasols
S'en alla un parapluie.

Ils se rencontrèrent
Devant la frontière.

— Viens sur ma toupie !
Dit le parapluie.

— Entre sur mon sol !
Dit le parasol.

Voilà pourquoi depuis,
Entre soleil et pluie,

La frontière nouvelle
Est un grand arc-en-ciel.

Umbrella and Parasol

Into Umbrella-land there flew
A Parasol. Ditto, likewise,

Flew an Umbrella through the skies
En route to Parasol-land too.

The pair met at their lands' frontier,
Greeted each other: "Come, my dear,"

Invites Umbrella, "visit me..."
And Parasol: "Please come and see

My spinning realm..." And that is why,
After a storm, spanning the sky,

Spreads a vast rainbow, to divide
Its rainy from its sunny side.

Crottin canin

Sur les trottoirs,
Les cabots trottent,
Les cabots trottent,
Trottent les chiens.

Sur les trottoirs,
Les cabots crottent,
Les cabots crottent,
Crottent les chiens.

Et je slalome
— Suivez le guide ! —
Entre boudins et pyramides.

Doggy Doo and Puppy Poo

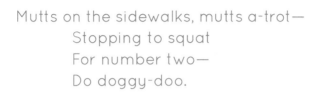

Mutts on the sidewalks, mutts a-trot—
    Stopping to squat
    For number two—
    Do doggy-doo.

Pups on the sidewalks, pups a-trot—
    Stopping to squat
    For number two—
    Poop puppy-poo.

    And, slalom-wise,
    Me: "Mind the guide!"
Zigzagging round, from side to side—
Here a turd-sausage, there a mound—
    Keeping my eyes
    Fixed on the ground!

Comptine desmois

JANVIER ouvre le bal.

FEVRIER : carnaval.

MARS, AVRIL : giboulées.

MAI muguet, JUIN cerise,

JUILLET, AOÛT sans chemise.

SEPTEMBRE : la rentrée,

OCTOBRE : le grand vent,

NOVEMBRE : la Toussaint,

DECEMBRE : le sapin.

Le premier jour de l'an
Tout repart comme avant.

"Eeny Meeny MONTHLY Moe" *

JANUARY starts the show.

FEBRUARY: Mardi Gras—

Sport (all sort!) and... Ooh là là!

MARCH, APRIL: squalls of sleet and snow.

MAY: lilies, JUNE: see cherries grow.

JULY and AUGUST: shirtless weather.

SEPTEMBER: back to school together.

OCTOBER: autumn leaves blow free.

NOVEMBER, All Saints' Day—amen!

DECEMBER: Look! The Christmas tree!

Then New Year's Day. And that is when
The whole show will begin again.

---

* A *comptine* is a French children's counting-rhyme, like the iconic

Am, stram, gram
Pic et pic et colégram,
Bour et bour et ratatam,
Am, stram, gram.

Le pagivore

Il eut soudain grand faim de livres,
En avala cent trente-trois

Dont un traité de savoir-vivre,
Mi à l'envers, mi à l'endroit.

Il épargna la poésie,
Dévora l'encyclopédie

Et juste à l'heure du dessert,
Mi à l'endroit, mi à l'envers,

Croqua la bibliothécaire.

The Librivore

Book glutton, hungering suddenly,
Gorged on a hundred thirty-three— *

One of them, on society's
Good table manners, if you please!—

(Half right side up, half upside down)
Devouring every verb and noun...

With little love of poetry,
He gulped the *Encyclopédie*... **

And when there is no more to sup,
For his dessert (half right side up,

Half upside down), his gut *livresque*
Gluts on librarian at her desk.

---

* The author admits unabashedly that the precise number of books was arrived at strictly for the rhyme.
** I take the liberty, with permission, of specifying here the celebrated voluminous Enlightenment monument, treating all manner of subject intellectual artistic, social, philosophical, and scientific, compiled between 1751 and 1782 by Diderot, d Alembert, and scores of other scholars. Our *librivore* would have enjoyed it as being far more straightforwardly prosaic than poetic.

Le requin

Un requin était triste :
Il avait mal aux dents.

Du fauteuil du dentiste,
Le requin sort content

Si content

Qu'il croque le dentiste
Sans avoir mal aux dents.

Le requin n'est plus triste :
Il mange comme avant.

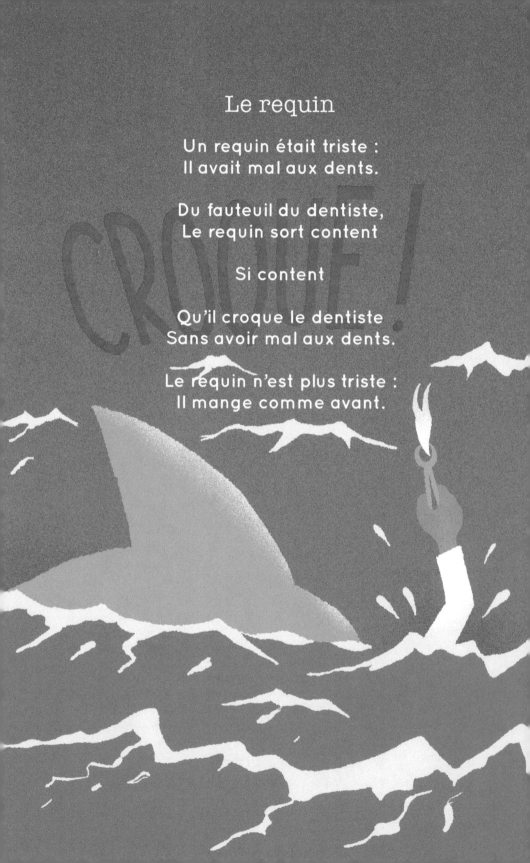

The Shark

A shark who'd had
A toothache—sad

And meal bereft—
Was cured. He left

The dental chair
And, joyously,

Saw dentist there...
Now, toothache-free,

Our predator:
One gulp—no more!—

Success!

Gluts as before,
And dentist-less!

A la une

A la une,
Je pars pour la Lune.

A la deux,
Je scrute les cieux,

A la trois,
Grimpe sur le toit.

A la sept,
Voici la comète.

A la cent,
Je monte dedans.

A la mille,
Je file, je file

Dans mon lit, mon île,
Jusqu'à midi pile

Number One, To and Fro [*]

Number one,
To and fro,
Off to the moon I go.

Number two,
On the rise.
My eyes inspect the skies.

Number three,
Tether-proof.
Aloft, I reach the roof...

Number seven,
And I see
A comet streak toward me.

A hundred,
And next minute,
I up and settle in it...

A thousand,
And I fly
Still higher, to the sky—

In my bed, my cocoon,
And huddle there till noon...

---

* The poet tells me that this rhyme is meant to accompany a child's imagined—or dreamed?—play on a swing, while postponing the need to leave the comfort of bed.

Puzzle

Ecris en grand
Le mot   **roman**

Découpe-le en cinq morceaux
Que tu mélanges aussitôt.

Étale le **a**, le **m**, le **o**,
Puis juste avant le **r**,
Mets le **n** à l'envers.

Colle les lettres, tour à tour,
Et tu obtiens le mot :

amour

Word Game

Print the word **NOVEL,** large, in caps. *
Cut it in pieces—five perhaps;
Mix them together, randomly...

Now take the **L**, the **O**, the **V**,
Spread them out, each to each, no gaps...

Erase the **N** and place the **E**.
What do you have? Easy to see:
No ***nove***lty!

What novels' pages tell us of:
That one word:

LOVE *

---

* I take the liberty of specifying "in caps", though Coran's original demands lowercase letters, given the particularity of the n, an upside-down u.
** I make a leap of interpretation here. Clearly, not all novels are love stories. But love, in some variety or other, does seem to play a role in most.

Le pygmée

J'ai couru
Comme un pygmée,
Les pieds nus
Dans la rosée.

C'était gai !
C'était gai !

J'étais léger,
Léger, léger
Comme une plume

Mais aujourd'hui,
Je suis au lit
Avec un rhume.

Pygmy-may-care

I frolicked through
The morning dew,
Devil-may-care,
Pygmy-like... Fleet
　　My feet,
　　And bare...

　　Delight!
　　Delight!

So light was I,
Light as a feather!

But now, tonight,
Tonight, oh my!
In bed I lie,
Under the weather.

La cane et la banane

De la basse-cour,
Une cane accourt.

Pressée, elle glisse
Sur une banane,

Dérape et se visse
Le bec dans l'avoine.

Calmée, la cane casse-cou
A une canne de bambou.

The Duck and the Banana Peel

A duck, making her way
Out of the *poulailler,*
Slipped ignominiously

On a banana peel,
Beak first, into a crop

Of oats, a-quack non-stop...
Once done her squawk and squeal,

Now no more raising Cain,
No more hullabaloo...

Our clumsy duck will deign
Carry a cane of stout bamboo.

C, N, H, E, I

Va pêcher dans l'alphabet,
Retire de tes filets
Trois consonnes, deux voyelles

Et tu construis, grâce à elles,
Sans scie, sans clou, sans machine,
La *niche* d'un *chien* de *Chine*.

Of Word and Wood

French consonants and vowels can be
Infinitely arranged. (I guess!) *
Indeed, with but two of the latter
And, of the former, only three,
You can see, it's a simple matter...

With no great skill—little or less!—
I can take C, N, H, I, E...
No saw, tool, hammer, nails, or screws
That any good wood-smith would use
(Or word-smith choose) to fashion it
Into a cozy canine scene,
Wrought out of word and wood! To wit,
"A *NICHE pour un CHIEN de CHINE.*"

Meaning? No need to look it up:
"A doghouse for a Chinese pup..." **

---

* With little mathematical certainty to support my allegation, I
think it best to defend it with this disclaimer.
** If my version seems too long compared to Coran's, I plead
"translator's extenutating circumstances," given the demands im-
posed by the linguistic divide, by his meaning, his rhymes—and by
my own self-serving enjoyment.

Chatte, chats

Do, do, ré, mi,
La chatte a mis

Fa, sol, la, si,
Des bigoudis.

Do, ré, mi, fa, sol, la, si, do,
Tous les chats lui font le gros dos.

Do, si, la, sol, fa, mi, ré, do,
La chatte a fui sous le piano.

Tchao ! Ciao !

Glamor-Puss and the Tomcats

Do, re, mi, fa... Do, re, mi, fa...
To give herself a pretty air,

Mi, fa, sol, la... Mi, fa, sol, la...
Kitty puts curlers in her hair.

Do, re, mi, fa, sol, la, si, do...
The toms all sneer and let her know,

Do, re, mi, fa, sol, la, si, do...
          Where she can go!

Whereat the glamor-pussycat
          Goes scooting, scat!
And hides under the piano now.

          Ciao! Tchao!

Questions sans réponse

Quand la forêt miaule
Dans le vent de l'été,

Est-ce l'oiseau d'un saule
Qui joue à chat perché ?

*

Une luciole est-elle
La lune des fourmis,
Celle des sauterelles,
Des papillons de nuit ?

*

Pourquoi en sa grotte humide,
La chauve-souris vit-elle là
Avec la tête en bas ?
Est-elle à ce point timide ?

Questions with No Answers

When forest meows
In summer breeze,

Does a bird on the willow boughs
Play "Catch-Cat Tag" among the trees? *

*

Does firefly seem to be
A moon to earth-bound ants,
To katydids a-hopping high,
To moths in flittering dance?

*

Why, in her murky grotto deep,
Do we see hanging there, asleep—
Lurking, head low—the bat?
Can she be timid as all that?

---

* I admit that this appellation for the venerable game of tag, is my
own attempt to relate it, believably, to its usual French equivalent,
le chat perché, in which the victim—"it"—is referred to as the "cat."

Palindrome

Eve

Anna

Ubu

Otto

Bob

Aziza :

Famille Palindrome,
Famille trouble-fête

Aux prénoms
Sans queue ni tête.

The Palindromes

The Palindromes, odd family:
Anna,
      and *Otto,*
           Bob,
               Aviva,
        Eve... (No, not *Eva!*)— *
Back and forth, forth and back—assails
The ear and eye, especially...

      Both heads and tails!

---

* The palindrome aficionado hardly needs this note to explain that the name Eva is not a gratuitous choice dictated by the rhyme.

Sauve-qui-peut

Sous la mangeoire,
Un ramier boite,
Traîne la patte.

Matin et soir,
Je le nourris

De pain,
De riz.

Quand il le faut, comme il convient,
J'arrose les chats des voisins.

Scat, Cats!

Under the feeder,
A dove, footsore,
Limping and lame, can move no more.

Day, night, I feed her—
Rice, bread crumbs... And

When neighbors' cats—marauding band—
Come stalk their prey,

I spray the lot... Shoo them away...

Qui tond ?

Une biche tond
Tond l'herbe du fond,
Du fond du jardin.

Je n'ai plus besoin,
Besoin de tondeuse,
Tondeuse à gazon.

Si demain, peureuse,
La biche me craint
Et me fait faux bond,

J'achète un mouton.

Mower and Mower

Nibbling, a doe
Has learned to mow
My garden grass.

And though, alas,
She nibbles slower
Than a lawn-mower,

Who needs the latter
With all its clatter?

If she should be
Scared off, and she
Escapes, a-leap,
Who cares? Not me!

I'll buy a sheep.

Baliverne

Est
Benêt,

Est
Niais,

Est
Nigaud,

Celui qui
Te dit que
Tu es né

Nu

Dans le chaud
D'un chou-cabus.

Twaddle

Simpleton is,

Dolt is,

Dunce is,

Whoever tells that tale of his
That once you sprouted, born and bare,

There,

In a batch
Of cabbage, in a cabbage patch. *

---

* Readers probably do not need to be reminded of the legend of babies' vegetal birth, that competed with the stork and chimney, and that was brilliantly, if somewhat unscrupulously, marketed into the worldwide rage of the Cabbage Patch Dolls of the 1980s.

Le panda

Pansu est le panda,
Panda venu de Chine

Qui se dodine et dîne
De pousses de bambou.

Le gourmand embobine
Le gardien du Jardin

Et pour sa faim de loup,
Vite, il emmagasine

Les bourgeons de cuisine
Dont tout panda est fou.

Il cache son trésor
Entre gong et pagode,

Loin des badauds qui rôdent
Puis d'un seul coup, s'endort.

---

* I had intended to suggest that this name, sounding typically pan-da-esque, may have been arrived at by conflating those of three celebrated pandas, Pan Dee, Pan Dah, and Su Sen, brought to the United States by Madame Chiang Kai-shek at the beginning of the war with Japan. Or even those of two other celebrated examples, Pan Pan and Su Lin. Before going out on that erudite limb, however,

The Panda

The Chinese panda, named Pan Su, *
Dawdled the livelong day away,

Dining on young shoots of bamboo,
Gorging them down galore. The zoo

Caretaker—woe and welladay!—
Had little choice, but quickly found

Himself to be wound tightly round
The panda's claw, eager to do

His bidding diet-wise. What's more,
The latter stuffs away a store

Of buds in the pagoda wall,
Next to the gong, far from the crowd

Of gaping louts who, long and loud,
Admire the doughty beast, and keep

"Ooh"ing and "aah"ing, one and all...
Pan Su just yawns, and falls asleep.

I was informed by the poet that he was inspired by his visits to the popular Belgian zoo of Pairi Daiza (originally Paradisio), since 1993 home especially to exotic species, and whose panda was delightfully pot-bellied—*pansu* in French... So much for the dangers of literary interpretation!

Six cent six cerises sures

Sur un lit de sucre blanc,
Six cent six cerises sures

Vont être changées — c'est sûr ! —
En gelée, en confiture

A moins que le cueilleur veille
A offrir aux quatre vents
Trois cent trois pendants d'oreilles.

Six hundred six sour cherries *

Six hundred six sour cherries lie
Pat on a bed of sugar, that

Will join them in a kitchen vat,
Turn them to jelly, by and by...

Unless half of their number—bangles
Hanging from lady's earlobes—dangles,
Cherry-picked, and fly, flung aside, **
Cast on the four winds, far and wide.

---

* The title of this vignette is part of a well-known tongue-twist-
er frequently conflated with another, in which the adjective *sures*
("sour") is confused with *sûres* ("certain"), producing an almost
equally rather meaningless result: "Ces cerises sont si sûres qu'on
ne sait pas si c'en sont."
** I ask the perceptive reader's indulgence for taking the liberty of
inserting a pun here that doesn't occur in the original.

Drôles d'R

Sans eau,
Sans air,

Plus de vie sur terre.

Sans o,
Sans r,

L'or n'est que poussière.

Sans zoo,
Sans aire,

— Là, c'est la galère
Au cirque, l'hiver,

Se lamente un clown
Sur Twitter.

Eau, Eau! What Airs?

Eau, eau! What airs?

        French letter-names
        Play funny games!

R is pronounced like *air,* and lo!
O sounds like *eau*—"water," you know...

Without them, life is finished, through:
No O, no R? Gold turns to dust!

Sans O (sans eau)... Sans O (sans zoo)... *

Waterless? Yes... And zoo-less too!
        Puzzled, nonplussed,
What can an animal trainer do?

        —Or, matter of fact,
        A circus act—

As clown complains, in accents bitter,
        Tweeting on Twitter...

---

* Students of French should recall that, despite its spelling, and unlike its English equivalent, *zoo* is pronounced to rhyme with *eau*.

Le nomade

Soir et matin,

Il glisse sans skis, sans patins
Sur la rosée, la boue.
Sa caravane n'a pas de roue.

Piano
Piano
Pianissimo,

Comme il en bave, l'escargot !

The Gypsy

Morning and night,
He skims the dew,
Ski-less and skate-less, oh so light
Of tread...
Wheel-less his caravan, he slithers through
The murky space, mud-deep, muck-spread,

So slow
So slow
Pianissimo...

Drooling, the snail plods on ahead.

La baleine de mon chapeau

A la claire fontaine,
Je vais puiser de l'eau,

De l'eau pour la baleine
Qui vit dans mon chapeau,

Dans mon chapeau de laine,
De laine de chameau.

Depuis, à la fontaine,
L'eau ne s'écoule plus :

Ma baleine a tout bu.

The Whale in My Hat

To crystal fountain off I'll go
Fetch water for the whale who, lo!

Lives in my hat—a fine chapeau
Of camel's hair *de luxe.* But oh!

Fountain sinks low in nothing flat:
Its crystal water, just like that,

Runs dry with one last gurgle, *splaaat!*
My thirsty whale, cup after cup,

Drank the whole crystal fountain up.

Le caillou

J'ai un caillou
Dans mon soulier
Qui me fait mal,
Très mal au pied.

J'ai un caillou
Dans mon soulier
Mais tant pis si
J'ai mal au pied.

J'ai, voyez-vous,
Beaucoup trop peur
Que le caillou
Soit dans mon cœur.

The Pebble

I have a pebble in my shoe,
That aches and smarts. But what to do?
My foot hurts, pains me through and through...

I have a pebble in my shoe,
That smarts and aches. But what to do?
Blast! Does my foot sting through and through?

Well, so it goes... I'm telling you,
Better "the horse before the cart!"
Best that the woes of ache and smart
Be in my foot... and not my heart.

L' Esquimau

Dans son igloo,
L'Esquimau fait
Des mots croisés.

Il trouve tout :
Les courts, les longs
Mais se surveille :

Son igloo fond
Dès qu'il écrit
Le mot « *soleil* ».

The Eskimo

Off in the Arctic snow,
An iglooed Eskimo
Works on a crossword puzzle,
Careful lest what he does 'll
Result—Ah! Negligence!—
In direst consequence...

He solves it all—
Big words and small.

But when he writes the last word: "sun",
The igloo melts. The puzzle's done.

L'âne de Norvège

Un âne avait si mal au dos
Qu'il mit des skis à ses sabots

Et son traîneau devint léger
Comme une feuille d'oranger.

C'était un âne de Norvège
Trop vieux pour trotter dans la neige.

Quand le pays chassa l'hiver,
Fondit en larmes, devint vert,

L'âne libéra ses sabots
Et s'en alla au petit trot

Apprendre aux ânons des vallées
Comment un âne peut skier.

The Norwegian Ass

An ass's back so painful proves
That he puts skis under his hooves.

His sled moves freer, lighter now
Than a leaf from an orange-bough!

(Old ass Norwegian, he was not
Able to trudge through snow a-trot.)

In time, when land grew winterless,
And spring tears greened its emptiness,

The ass took off his skis and went
About with but one new intent:

To teach young asses how to ski
Mountain passes Norwegianly...

Le petit poisson doré

Il a tant et tant pleuré,
Le petit poisson doré
Que le vase a débordé.

Et l'eau a coulé, coulé
Emportant le prisonnier
Vers le ruisseau du verger.

Aujourd'hui, dans la rivière,
Il promène, heureux et fier,
Ses écailles de lumière.

The Little Goldfish

A little goldfish yearned to be
Freed from his bowl, and sadly he
Wept bitter tears... So copiously,

That soon they overflowed, and poured
Down to the brook, carried him toward
A life of freedom: rich reward!

Now glows the goldfish, all a-shimmer,
Happy at last... Flits free... Bold swimmer,
Proud to parade scales' golden glimmer...

Acrostiche pascal

Cieux

Herbe

Œufs

Cloches

Oh ! oh !

La chasse

Aux cadeaux

Taïaut !

Easter Acrostic

Cloudless sky...

High and low,

On the lawn,

Children go

Off... Press on,

Looking—oh!—

As eggs hide...

Tally-ho!

Eastertide...

Balade

J'ai suivi les sentiers
Qui coupent la forêt,

Vu fuir sous les genêts
Un renard sans sa ruse,

Offert à une buse
Un abat de poulet

Et surtout respiré,
En fin de promenade,

L'air mouillé des cascades
Qui cerise le nez.

Stroll

I took a forest stroll
From wooded knoll to knoll;

Watched as a fox—without
His bag of tricks, to flout

His prey—lay in the grass;
Fed buzzard with a bunch

Of chicken bones, from lunch...
And, as it came to pass

That my stroll now was through,
Breathed the cascades' moist air

That turns a cherry hue
Men's noses everywhere.

Le rhinocéros

Un rhinocéros
Rêve d'une brosse

Qui lui laverait
Les yeux et le nez,

Qui lui laverait
Le dos, les oreilles.

Le rhinocéros
Qui n'a pas de brosse

Ne nettoie jamais
Ses yeux ni son nez,

Ne nettoie jamais
Son dos, ses oreilles.

Il se dore au soleil.

The Rhinoceros

Rhinoceros—
No fret, no fuss—

Yearns, dreams about
A brush to wash

His eyes, his snout,
A brush to wash

His ears, his back...
Brushless, alack!

He cannot wash
His eyes, his snout,

His ears, his back.
He cannot wash

At all, by gosh!
Rhino, forsooth—

Unbrushed, uncouth,
Unwashed, alas!—

Sunbathes, a-glitter on the grass.

Pourquoi la patate
a-t-elle des yeux ?

— Pourquoi la patate
   A-t-elle des yeux ?

     — Pour plaire aux tomates,
       Aux grillons frileux,
       Aux vers acrobates
       Sans tête ni queue ?

— Pourquoi la patate
   A-t-elle des yeux ?

     — Pour servir de feux
       Aux convois pirates
       D'escargots peureux
       Et de mille-pattes ?

— Si une patate
   N'avait pas ses yeux,
   N'en déplaise au ciel
   Et aux taupes grises

     Comment pourrait-elle
     Ôter sa chemise ?

Why Do Potatoes Have Eyes?

Why do potatoes—yams, no less—
        Have eyes?   *

                I guess,
To please tomatoes, crickets a-shiver,
Craven and chill, lily of liver,
And headless worms—and tail-less—who
Wreak acrobatic derring-do.

Why do potatoes—yams, no less—
        Have eyes?

                I guess,
        To warn piratic
        Corsairs aquatic,
Snails in a dither, millipedes too—
Feet all a-slither—more than a few!

For, if potatoes had no eyes—
And yams no less—I theorize,
But certainly don't mean to scoff!
Blind as a mole, what ever could,

        What ever would
They do to get their jackets off? **

---

* Not certain if Coran is referring here, familiarly, to the *pomme de terre*, with a term equivalent to the English "spud," or, indeed, to the yam-like sweet potato, I resolve my doubt by including both.
** Throughout my childhood I was always cajoled to eat my potatoes with the assurance that "Potatoes with their jackets on are fit for dukes and kings," a bit of folklore no doubt inherited by my parents from theirs.

Les moustiques

Les moustiques
Piquent, piquent
Les gens qui
Pique-niquent.

Ils attaquent
En oblique
Les hamacs
Elastiques

Et bivouaquent,
Sans panique,
Dans les sacs
En plastique.

Les moustiques
Font la nique
Aux gens qui
Pique-niquent

Et qu'ils piquent
Et repiquent
En musique.
Pas comique !

The Mosquitos

Mosquitos bite,
Mosquitos sting
People who might
Be picnicking.

They dive, a-wing...
As hammocks sway
And swing away,
They bite and sting...

They camp by day,
They camp by night,
Calmly delight
In trash-bag play...

Mosquitos sting,
Sneer, buzz, and bite
People who might
Be picnicking.

They buzz, bite, sting,
Harass the latter.
Some say they sing!
No laughing matter...

Menu Menu

Un céleri,
Deux salsifis,
Trois échalotes,

Quatre radis,
Ail et persil,
Une biscotte,

Cœur de poireau
Epinards frais,
Carottes crues,

Riz cuit à l'eau,
Du pain au lait,
De la laitue :

C'est le festin végétarien
De la tortue de mon copain.

A feast? A fast...

One stalk of celery.
Two sprigs of salsifis,
Shallots too, but just three,

Parsley, radishes four,
Garlic—one clove, no more!—
Fresh spinach leaves galore,

Raw carrots, twice-baked bread, *
Heart of leek, on a bed
Of lettuce—a whole head...

Dessert? Milk-toast! (And not **
To be forgot, a pot
Of steaming rice, boiled hot...)

This feast of vegetarian treats
Is what my friend's pet turtle eats.

---

* I freely translate *biscotte*—the popular world-wide *zweiback* or
zwieback, a kind of rusk—according to its Germanic etymology:
"twice-baked."
** I take the liberty of interpreting Coran's *pain au lait*, milk-toast,
as the common *pain perdu*, roughly the equivalent of our French
toast but usually a sweet dessert served with fruit.

Le castor

Quand la maison s'endort,
Je me change en castor
Et grignote des mots
Par la tête ou le dos :

La NOUILLE de la greNOUILLE,
La SOLE de la bousSOLE
Et le POIS de POISson.

La COUPE de la souCOUPE,
La CROÛTE de la chouCROÛTE
Et le BOIS de BOISson.

Devines-tu pourquoi
Je ne grignote pas
Mais jette
Les cacahuètes ?

The Beaver *

When sleeping lies the house and all is still,
    I change myself into a beaver,
And with my two front teeth—my double cleaver!—
Nibble on certain words, frontwards or back.

    And so I hew and hack until,
        With my attack,
MOUSE falls from MOUSEtrap (wishing mice no ill!).
I saw and rip HONEY from HONEYdew,
Gnaw BUTTERCUP, leave BUTTER, lap my fill...
    Ditto with CHEESE from CHEESEcloth too,

    And slice BREAD from BREADwinner
        With my dinner,
Separate PILLbox, swallow many a PILL!...

    But I am certain you can bet
    Exactly why I never will
Split up French peanuts (known as CACAhuètes)!

---

* I hope the reader needs no note to defend my preservation of
the general idea and tone of this poem despite the impossibility of
retaining its idiosyncratic specifics—except, that is, for the closing
words.

Le chameau

Un chameau entra dans un sauna.

Il eut chaud,
Très chaud,
Trop chaud.

Il sua,
Sua,
Sua.

Une bosse s'usa,
S'usa,
S'usa.

L'autre bosse ne s'usa pas.

Le chameau, dans le désert,
Se retrouva dromadaire.

The Camel

A camel in a sauna got
All hot,
Hot,
Hot

With sweat,
Sweat,
Sweat,

Until one hump,
One hump,
One hump,

Melted... And yet
Hump number two

Remained as it was meant to do:

The desert beast, now weak and wary,
Had turned into a dromedary.

Saperlipopette

Saperlipopette!

Le paon de mon voisin
Se croit une vedette.

En haut d'un tambourin,
Il joue des castagnettes,
Ouvre son éventail

Et crie des *aïe ! aïe ! aïe !*
A s'en rougir le col :
C'est un paon espagnol.

A Peacock's Tale

"Ye gods and little fishes!" *

My neighbor's peacock wishes
To play the fine *vedette.*

With tambourine and castanet,
He spreads his tail against the sky,
And crows many an "ay ay ay!"
          A-click, a-clack.

     Flushed egomaniac,
          This dancer manic...
          Peacock Hispanic!

---

* Obviously, I render the line, which also serves as Coran's original
title, with a similarly meaningless English exclamation.

Papillon de jour

Papillon de jour,
Quand le soleil court,

Tu voles
Et voles
Et voles
Parmi les corolles.

Tu es le facteur,
Le facteur des fleurs.

Mais dis-moi, quand la lune luit,
Où vont les papillons de nuit ?

Daytime Butterfly

Butterfly in the bright
Day's light... But moth by night...

You fly
And fly
And fly
Among the petals.

Day's butterfly... To flowers you bring
Messages flitting on the wing.

But nighttime moth? When daylight settles
Into the night, and dark the sky,
When glows the moon, where do you go?
Where? Who's to know?

Compliment

En ce nouveau printemps,

Je te fêterai,
Maman,

Je te fêterai,
Papa

Mais pas en même temps
Et pas le même jour.

Et pourtant,

Le cœur qui bat en moi
Bat pour un même amour.

Days of Praise

Another year, another spring...

And I will sing
Your name, mammá,,

And I will sing
Your name, papá...

Heartfelt, my praise,
Though I sing each on different days! *

And yet,

This heart I'm speaking of,
Beats—you can bet—
All at once, with one selfsame love.

---

* Occurring throughout the world on different dates in different countries, the French *Fête des Méres* and *Fête des Pères*, equivalent of our Mother's Day and Father's Day are usually celebrated in late May and late June respectively.

Origami

Papier mouillé
Qui dégouline,

Papier teinté
D'encre de Chine,

Papier plié et aspergé
D'un fond de tasse de café,

Papier séché
Sur chevalet

Et le chef-d'œuvre
Est une pieuvre.

Origami

Paper, all dripping wet, flat laid...

Paper, ink-tinged, the blackest shade...

Paper folded, coffee-dregs-sprayed...

Paper drying, on easel spread...

My masterpiece... What's this I did?
           What have I made?

An octopus? A giant squid?
           Eight limbs... Huge head...

Trio

Trois coqs courent dans le jardin.

Le premier coq est muet,
Le deuxième est enrhumé,
Le dernier s'est envolé.

Aucun des trois n'a chanté.

Le jour ne s'est pas levé
Et le soleil est resté
Dans son lit.

Moi aussi.

Trio

Three garden cocks go strutting round.

> The first can't make a sound,
> The second has a cough,
> The last one just flew off.

Not one crowed "cock-a-doodle-doo!"

> Result? Dawn—sleepyhead!—
> Sleeps in. Sun stays in bed.

> Me too.

À Copenhague

La petite sirène,
Certains soirs, se promène.
Personne ne sait où.

Selon un vieux coucou,
Elle irait effeuiller,
Effeuiller une rose

Sur la pierre
Où son père,
Andersen, se repose.

In Copenhagen

Some evenings, furtively,
The little mermaid leaves the sea,
Though where she goes
Nobody knows.

But an old cuckoo claims that she
Visits a grave and strews a rose's
Petals—here, there—
On the tomb where
Her father, Andersen, reposes. *

---

* Readers will easily recognize the allusion to Hans Christian Andersen's famous Danish fairy tale "The Little Mermaid," originally published in 1837 and reworked over the years in a vast array of languages and media—literary, musical, and dramatic—the statue of whose heroine, a favorite tourist attraction, has graced the harbor at Copenhagen since 1914.

Chaud chow – chow

Peu lui chaut
Au chow-chow

S'il a chaud,
Chaud,
A chaud aux oreilles

Quand il fait son show,
Le chow-chow,
Sous le chaud soleil.

Chow Chow

Chow-Chow cares not
A rap or jot

How hot
He's got...

Ears and the rest!
For when the "Best
Of Show" is judged, of all the lot,
Chow-Chow the Chow is number one
Under the sun!

Mots d'école

Tous les livres d'école
Sont pleins de mots bizarres
Qu'il faut bien qu'on se colle
Au fond de la mémoire :

TROGLODYTE CRO-MAGNON
MAMMOUTH IGUANODON
BRONTOSAURE TUMULUS
SILEX DIPLODOCUS
DYNAMO DYNAMITE
COSMOS MÉTÉORITE
BICÉPHALE QUADRUPÈDE
PARALLÉLÉPIPÈDE.

Pas faciles à comprendre,
Pas faciles à apprendre,
À moins de les trouver
Amusants à chanter.

School Words *

The books we use in school are very
Full of abstruse vocabulary,
Words that defy our mental focus;
Words that would fill a syllabary
With letters supernumerary;
Words that take mental hocus-pocus
For us to learn... Words that could choke us:

TROGLOYTE and **IGUANADON.**
BICEPHALOS, BOUSTREPHODON,
DIPLO´DOCUS (or **DIPLODO´CUS**?)...
Words that it's pointless to pretend
That we can really comprehend;
Words like **EDUCE, PERCUSE, ACCLUSE**...
Words that we can find no excuse—
Like **REPETEND** and **SUBTRAHEND**—
Try though we may, to introduce
Into our sage elucubrations,
Let alone daily conversations!

But rather than try mastering 'em,
We have more fun trying to sing 'em.

---

* As elsewhere (see for example, "The Beaver," p. 78–79), the reader will, I hope, appreciate the liberties imposed by the subject matter on a translator eager to transmit to some extent the spirit, tone, and even the sounds of Coran's original vignette.

Les judokas

Trois bonobos
En kimono
Ont fait du judo,

Tant et tant sauté,
Tant et tant tourné

Comme des toupies
Sur le tatami

Que tous ont depuis
Un torticolis.

The Judo Masters

Three judo masters—bonobos,
Kimono-clad—strike judo pose, *

      Turn, twist, leap, kick,
      Do every trick...

      But soon all three—oh!
      Yes, the whole trio—

    Display their artistry,
    Over the tatami, **

Until, by dint of tug and tussle,
None can so much as move a muscle.

---

* Admirers of Jane Goodall will remember affectionately that the bonobo is a Congolese variety of chimpanzee.
** The typical Japanese tatami is a soft woven mat used as a floor covering to sit on when taking meals, and also for performing various martial arts.

Ramdam

1, 2, 3,
Chien aboie.

4, 5, 6,
Porte crisse.

7,
Mobylette.

8 et 9,
Neuf teuf-teuf.

10 et 11,
Gongs de bronze.

12 et 13,
Boules Quies.

Noise Annoys

1, 2, 3,
Dog barks at me.

4, 5, 6,
Door creaks and sticks.

7, 8,
Harley's brakes grind, grate.

9, 10, 11,
Trains chug toward heaven,

12, 13,
Mach Ten flying machine.

14, 15 (and more),
Ear plugs from the corner store... *

---

* My and Coran's readers are too perceptive to need a note, except for those unfamiliar with a common brand of French ear plugs.

Le soleil sur mon lit

Le soleil a dormi,
A dormi sur mon lit.

Fin de nuit, tôt levé,
Il a quitté le lit

Et l'astre est retourné
Trôner dans l'infini.

Moi qui étais lacté
Des orteils au visage,

Depuis je suis bronzé
Comme un lézard de plage.

The Sun on My Bed

The sun, asleep,
Slept on my bed,

Till dawn, a-peep,
Arose... Then fled

Back to the sky,
Enthroned in it,

Ruling on high
The infinite.

And I, once pale from head
To toe, now proudly stand—

Beach-lizard, amply spread
With color, nicely tanned.

Point de mire

Le canard
A bu la mare.

Le canard
A bu la mer.

Puis il a croqué le mur
Et le canard en est mort.

*Confit*eor !

In View of All

A duck, a-thirst,
Sucks dry, at first,

The swamp. Then he
Sucks dry the sea!

Eventually, in view of all,
He chomps the wall,
And—live no more—
Is served up as *canard confit*.

Confiteor! *

---

* I remind any readers whose culinary and ecclesiastical vocabularies may be wanting, that the wordplay here is based on the resemblance between *canard confit* ("conserve of duck") and the *Confiteor* ("I confess") that introduces the rite of confession.

Le ver vu

Un vert vermisseau fait le beau
Sur une pile de vaisselle.

Il vient, il va
De verre en plat.

Le vert vermisseau ne voit pas
Que sa belle est un vermicelle.

When Worm Would Woo

On dinner table, all a-slither,
A long green worm, spaghetti-thin,

Primps, dish to dish, hither and thither,
His fervent wish—poor, simple fellow—
        To woo and win...

Our green worm doesn't know his belle—oh!—
Is just some diner's *vermicello.*

La sorciere du feu ouvert

La sorcière du feu ouvert
N'a que deux dents :

Une derrière,
Une devant,

Une qui hoche,
Une qui cloche.

Voilà pourquoi la sorcière
Qui vit dans le feu ouvert

S'empiffre, le jour, la nuit,
De bouillons et de bouillies,

D'asticots, de vers de terre,
De limaces, de chenilles

Et de patates pourries.
Pauvre fille !

The Witch Who Haunts the Hearth

The witch who haunts the hearth, in truth,
Is oh! so long—and short—of tooth.

> She has but two:
> One front, one back.

And, of the pair—alas, alack!—
Neither can bear what teeth should do:
> They cannot chew!

And that is why, by night, by day,
The hearthside witch laps mere purée,
Clear broths, soft stew of worms and bugs—

Moths, caterpillars, garden slugs,
Fetid spuds, molding, festering—
> Poor thing!

L'orang-outan

Sur une oasis,
Un orang-outan
Croque des oignons
Pour passer le temps.

Depuis, l'oasis
A changé d'odeur.
Sur le sable blond,
Tous les chameaux pleurent.

Chimp Chomps *

Oasis ground...
Chimp chomps away
On onions, round
The clock. All day...

Oasis... And
Foul stench widespread,
As camels shed
Tears in the sand...

---

* Primatologists among my readers will, I expect, excuse my poet-
ic license of changing Coran's orang-outang to a chimpanzee. Un-
less, that is, there is a dramatic difference in the taste for onions
among the formers and the latters. Interestingly, specialists are in
sharp disagreement regarding the positive or negative effects of
onions in the animals' diet.

Riz et rats

Riz
Dans le ru.

Rats
A l'affût.

Riz dévoré,
Rats rassasiés.

Corbeaux ravis
D'avoir raté,

Raté le riz
Des trois raviers,

Raviers remplis,
Remplis à ras

De mort-aux-rats.

Rice and Rats

Rice
Floods the ground,

Rats
Flock, abound.

Rats gorge until
They glut their fill.

Crows' appetite
Remains un-sated.

Humiliated,
Still they delight:

Let it suffice
To say the rice

Was amply laced—
Full to the brim—

With death, posthaste,
To life and limb:

Rat-poison paste!

La souris et l'hurluberlu

Quel est l'hurluberlu,
Le fichu m'as-tu-vu

Qui a jugé bon
De donner mon nom

A un bouton à roulette
Qui cliquette sur le Net

Sans que personne
Ne s'en étonne ?

Et le pire :
Même les chats
N'en veulent pas.

C'est tout dire !

The Mouse and the Fathead

Who was that fathead fool
Who thought my name was cool

To give a keyboard app
That lets them play roulette,

Click-clack, over the Net?
Who even gave a rap?

    Stupidity!
    If you ask me,

    He was all wet!
    And cats agree.

    So Q.E.D.

Danseur étoile

Un escargot
Tournait en rond
Sur un savon.

Plus l'escargot tournait,
Plus le savon s'usait.

Plus le savon s'usait,
Plus il devenait bulles.

L'escargot, dans les bulles,
Se sentit ridicule.

Alors, à reculons,
Il quitta le savon

Et partit tel un Tsigane
Promener sa caravane.

Snail Two-Step

A snail was slithering circles on
A cake of soap... Round, round... Anon,

The more said snail crawled roundabout,
The more the soap went petering out.

The more the soap went petering out,
The more would bubbles fill the air,

Until our snail—bubble-bound there,
Feeling the fool—turned tail and quit *
Said soap, lest he appear a twit,

Backed off and, Gypsy-like, began
Hauling away his caravan...

---

* To readers who object that snails really have no proper tails, I
reply that the metaphorical expression is often used with no liter-
al intent, as when Napoléon, after the Russian campaign, "turned
tail" and retreated, his tail between his legs, so to speak.

Le bourlingueur

Il prit sa brosse à dents,
Son sac de faux croco,
Une flûte de Pan,

Un pot d'encre de Chine,
Un pinceau, un stylo
Et du papier machine.

Impatient d'être en l'air,
Il courut, ventre à terre,
Jusqu'à l'aéroport.

C'était la grève des transports.

The Adventurer

He packs his bag—faux alligator—
Makes sure to take his toothbrush (and
His pan-pipes to make music later),

His India ink, a brush, a pen,
Typing paper, a writing-stand...

Impatient to fly off again,
He takes himself a breathless hike,
Airport-bound, to his favorite
Airline, only to find that it

And all the rest have just gone out on strike.

Le dragon et la grue

Dans la rue,
Un dragon
Gros, grotesque et grognon

Agrippé au grappin
D'une grue
Se cramponne.

Mais là-haut, le dragon
Ne fait peur à personne :

Sur son mur de grès gris,
Il n'est qu'un *graffiti*.

The Dragon and the Crane *

Look! In the street,
A dragon! There...
(Fat, fearsome, peevish pose!
    Yet, goodness knows,
    Proper, discreet...)

    Clutches a pole—
    Crane in the air—

    But doesn't scare
    A living soul!

Chalked on the gray concrete—oh!—
He's only a *grafitto!* **

* With his typical whimsy, the poet, by his title, invites the reader
to expect a common fable scenario featuring two animals, only to
realize, as he reads, that the "crane" in question—in English as well
as French—is of the inanimate construction variety.
** For the punctilious reader, I strike a blow for linguistic accura-
cy by insisting on the grammatically correct but seldom (if ever)
used singular.

Le dinosaure

Dehors,
Dedans,

L'été durant,
Par tous les temps,

Mon dinosaure
N'est pas gênant.

Il tremble, il ronfle
S'il se dégonfle.

Rien d'étonnant, tu le devines,
Pour une bouée de piscine.

The Dinosaur

Outdoors
And in,
No matter what the weather's been,

My dinosaur's
Tame as can be,
All summer long.

In time, when he
Grows limp, he snores,

And shakes, and roars.
No, you're not wrong,

Not strange at all:
He's just a rubber bathtub-doll.

Le mouton

Un mouton s'amuse,
S'amuse à muser.

Un mouton s'amuse,
S'amuse à corner.

Le mouton qui corne,
Le mouton qui muse

Croit qu'il sait jouer,
Jouer désormais

De la cornemuse
Comme un Écossais.

The Sheep

A sheep takes pleasure,
Muses at leisure—

Amused, alone—
Or, when he's not

Lost deep in thought,
Doodles, a-drone, *

Musing how he
Toots musically,

Hoots like self-taught
Bag-piping Scot.

---

* For the curious reader, *doodle* is a Scottishism meaning, appropriately, to toot on the bagpipe (or drone). I hope the same reader will appreciate that, French vocabulary being what it is, Coran has an easier time with his wordplay on *muser* (to muse), *corner* (to hoot), and *cornemuse* (bagpipe) than do I. A common problem for any translator.

Cachotteries

Qui use ses chaussettes
Dans le Massachusetts ?

Qui traque les souris
Dans le Mississippi

Et dans le Missouri,
Les chats en appétit ?

Qui rappe et fait la manche
Devant la Maison Blanche ?

Qui escalade, poings liés,
La statue de la Liberté ?

Aux U.S.A., nul ne le sait.

Hush-hush

In Massachusetts, who
Wears socks till toes poke through?

Who, in Mississippi,
Tracks mice relentlessly?

And cats, whose hungry fury
Drives them on in Missouri?

Who, on the White House lawn,
Begs: "Spare change?" Raps till dawn?

Who, handcuffed, scales the proud, the free
Statue of Liberty?

In U. S. A.,
Who can say?

Heures

Heure d'hiver,
Heure d'été,

Heure d'été,
Heure d'hiver :

La Nature n'en a que faire.

Du grand soleil aux glaçons,
Elle anime, à sa façon,
Le manège des saisons.

Changing the Clock

Winter time,
Then summer time,

Summer time,
Then winter time:

Nature is not to blame! No rhyme,
No reason... Time, by sun controlled,
Plies seasons' path, from hot to cold,
Not merely by the tick and tock
Of humans' yearly-changing clock!

Si

Et si la pluie se voulait sage
Se blottissait en son nuage,

Si la neige en faisait autant
Et cessait son manège blanc,

Si les vents, les grêlons du ciel
Ne jouaient plus à la marelle,

Que deviendrait la Terre
Sous un soleil d'enfer ?

If

If rain, endowed with common sense,
Sat pat in its cloud residence;

If snow refused, by night, by day,
To while its frost-white hours away;

If wind and sky-borne hailstones found
It best to stop hopscotching round

The ground... How might earth live, undone,
Scorched hot under a hellish sun?

La puce et l'éléphant

Pour une puce,

Un éléphant,
C'est bien souvent
Un autobus,

Avec sa trompe,
Une autopompe

Ou à la rigueur,
Un aspirateur.

The Flea and the Elephant

For a flea,

An elephant—
Ambulant
And ponderous—
Seems to be
A city bus.

Or, using his
Trunk, he is—
Without the clothes—
A fireman's hose.

Whereas, for some,
His demeanor
Lets him become
A vacuum cleaner.

Dans mon zoo

Dans mon zoo,
Pas de barreau,

Pas de mur
Ni de clôture,

De collier,
De muselière.

Chacun fait
Ce qu'il lui plaît,

Du chameau
A la panthère,

Dans mon zoo
Imaginaire.

In My Zoo

In this, my zoo,
Beasts, free to spend

Days, nights, un-penned,
As beasts should do:

No cage, no wall
To hem them in...

No bars at all,
Without, within...

No collars—banned!—
No muzzles! And

Each roams about,
Within, without,

From panther to
The dromedary...

Here, in my zoo
Imaginary.

Cavale

Une dinde s'est enfuie
A travers prés et prairies.

— J'aime mieux, glougloute-t-elle,
Me faire la belle
Et courir le monde
Que finir rôtie,
Farcie, en quenelles

Dans un four immonde,
La nuit de Noël.

Turkey-Trot *

Gobbling, a turkey proudly said: "Oh,
See how I flee through field and meadow.

I'd rather primp and strut with pride,
Boasting my beauty far and wide,
Than end up as my sisters do,
Baking or roasting through and through,

Stuffed, in a nasty stove—would you believe?—
Or poached, as turkey stew, on Christmas eve!"

---

* With his typical good-natured indulgence, the poet has allowed
me to transform his title, implying simply "on the run," into the
energetic American ragtime dance of the twenties, which, in turn,
gave its name to modern charity road-races held in various cities
around Thanksgiving.

État-civil du Père Noël

Papa Noël
N'est pas papa.
Papa de qui ?

Papa Noël
N'est pas papy.
Papy de qui ?

Papa Noël
N'est pas papa,
N'est pas papy.

Il est — c'est clair ! —
Célibataire.

Father Christmas's Social Status

No, "Papa Christmas" shouldn't use
That name as his. A father? Whose?

No, "Papa Christmas" shouldn't mask
His name with "Grandpa." Whose, I ask?

No, "Papa Christmas?" Not his nature!
"Papa" or "Grandpa?" Neither, nor!
Why falsify his nomenclature?

What is the old man then? No more
Than a childless old bachelor...

Pour être magicien

Pour être magicien,
Pas besoin de baguette,
De costume à paillettes
Et de turban indien.

Pour être magicien,
Pas besoin de bricoles,
De feu, de fumerolles
Et de perlimpinpin.

Pour être magicien,
Il suffit d'une main
Au fond d'une chaussette
Qui devient marionnette.

Il suffit de cinq doigts
Qui parlent par ta voix,
Rien de plus, rien de moins
Pour être magicien.

To Be a Magician

Would you be a magician?
Is it your life's ambition?
No need for sequined clothes,
Wand, turbaned Hindu pose...

Would you be a magician?
Is it your wistful mission?
No need for fire, smoke, all
The fancy folderol...

Would you be a magician?
You need but one condition:
Five fingers in a sock
And a voice that can talk

Like puppet apparition...
That's all you need: a hand,
A tongue at your command—
Voilà! You're a magician!

abra
cada
bra!

Babiroussa

BA   BA

    BA   BA

BI   BI

    BI   BI

ROUSSA

BABIROUSSA :

C'est le solo chez les Malais
D'un cochon-cerf,
Brun sanglier
Un peu balèze,
Inconnu,
Méconnu
Mais connu
Au dictionnaire
Page 116.

Babirusa

BA   BA   B I   BI

Fa sol la si...

BI   BI   BA   BA

    An aria
    On creature Asian,
    Sung in Malaysian...
"Babirusa," its name. Stout beast
      That roams the East...
      Beast real or not?
      Tame? Wild? Un-caught.
      Unknown, unseen...
      Except for there!
   In *Le Petit Robert,*
      Page 116. *

---

* The poet informs me that he actually happened on the exot-ic word in that dictionary—whose French name, to reassure the formal purist, does rhyme with "there"—exact page or not. A real animal, in fact, its name—*babirusa* in English—is derived in French from the Malaysian compound of *babi* ("pig") and *rusa* ("deer"). It is common in several sub-species, especially in Indonesia.

Fichu taon

Un taon m'a piqué
Les joues et le nez,
M'a piqué le cou,
Un bras, un genou.

Et jamais, jamais,
— Vous pouvez me croire —
Jamais mon miroir
Ne m'a vu si laid.

Depuis, je perche
Sur un talus
A la recherche
Du taon perdu.

Time's Fly

A horsefly lights on me
And bites my cheeks, my nose,
My neck, and down it goes,
Biting an arm, a knee.

Never my looking-glass—
Surely you will concur—
Has rendered me, alas!
An image uglier!

Now, on this bank, I try—
Latter-day Proust, alone—
To catch time on the fly...
Time... Fly, fleet-flying... Flown... *

---

* My seemingly gratuitous allusion to Proust, beyond the ken of all but the most precocious child readers, should, thanks to the homonyms "taon" and "temps," be clear at least to literate adults.

En cage

Sur son perchoir
De bois gris noir,

Un perroquet
Chagrin, se tait,
Cache sa peine.

Il n'a plus envie de parler,
Il n'a plus la joie de voler.

Depuis des jours,
Son cœur est lourd
Comme sa chaîne.

Caged

The parrot, caged, is perched upon
A peg of dark gray wood. Dark too
His mood, alas! Sad, woebegone,

Distressed, depressed... But what to do?
His tongue is cackle-less, his wings,

Unmoved, fled their gay flutterings...
Gone, joyous urge to talk, to fly.

Each dismal day lolls idling by...
Heavy the chain that keeps him pent,
Heavy his heart, in bondage spent...

Souhait

Comme toi,

Je vais là où je veux,
Je cours comme je peux,
Je décolle,
Je m'envole
Et je franchis les mers
Aussi libre que l'air.

Comme toi,

Ca m'émeut de savoir
Qu'au sein du monde entier,
A l'ombre d'un pouvoir,
Des pays sont privés,
Privés de liberté.

Dans *poème*, on lit *aime*.
Que ce mot,
En écho,
Demain comme aujourd'hui,
Par ta voix, soit un cri.

Desire

Poet, like you...

Blithe, debonair,
I fly my fill...
Travel over the land, the sea,
Lithe as the air,
Wing where I will,
Unfettered, free.

Poet, like you...

It troubles me
To see that in this world of ours,
Bereft of love
And liberty,
People live in the dark shade of
Ignoble powers.

In *poetry* we can read *try*...
If only that word might apply
To love! Today,
Tomorrow too!
Try, poet, with your every cry,
To let it ring, loud as it may,
The whole world through! *

---

* I doubt it will be lost on Coran's (and my) readers that this final vignette in his collection, destined or not to be understood by the young, closes the parenthesis opened by the inspiration of the first, "To Write a Poem." Not an accident, we can suspect...

La poésie n'a pas de fin...

PIERRE CORAN (*pseud.* Eugène Delaisse) was born in 1934 in Saint-Denis en Brocqueroie, near Mons in Belgium. One of Belgium's preeminent French-language writers of children's literature, Coran is a prolific and award-winning writer of nearly 100 works of poetry, novels, screenplays, and essays. His work has been turned into films, plays, and television series. Coran's honors are many, among them the Prix Jean de La Fontaine in 1976, and the first Grand Prix de Poésie pour la Jeunesse in 1989. He has won every major literary award in Belgium and has been translated into a number of languages. His many works include recent titles *Fables à l'air du temps* (2014), *Fables des Villes et des Champs* (2018), and *AmuseRimes* (2019), all translated by Norman Shapiro and made available in the U.S. by Black Widow Press. Coran lives with his wife in the village of Jurbise, in the Walloon province of Hainaut.

NORMAN R. SHAPIRO (Ph.D., Harvard) is Distinguished Professor and Poet-in-Residence at Wesleyan University. A decorated Officier de l'Ordre des Arts et des Lettres de la République Française, he is a member of the Academy of American poets.

Among his award-winning translations are *Four Farces by Georges Feydeau* (Chicago), nominated for a National Book Award; *The Fabulists French: Verse Fables of Nine Centuries* (Illinois), the ALTA Distinguished Book of the Year; *One Hundred and One Poems by Paul Verlaine* (Chicago), recipient of the MLA's Scaglione Prize; and *Charles Baudelaire: Selected Poems from "Les Fleurs du mal"* (Chicago). He has also published three collections of La Fontaine's *Fables,* the first of which was chosen as the text for a luxury limited edition by The Folio Society of London (2013); the *Complete Fables of Jean de La Fontaine* (Illinois), recipient of the Galantière Prize, and a volume of La Fontaine's *contes, La Fontaine's Bawdy: Of Libertines, Louts, and Lechers* (Lockert Library of Poetry in Translation, Princeton); *Lyrics of the French Renaissance* (Yale); *Nine Centuries of French Women Poets* (Johns Hopkins). Recent volumes include poetry collections of Théophile Gautier (in Yale's Margellos World Republic of Letters series), Anna de Noailles, Sabine Sicaud, Jacques Prévert, Cécile Périn, three collections of Belgian poet Pierre Coran, as well as *Fe-Lines: French Cat Poems through the Ages* (Illinois). His series of French animal poetry, *Ménagerie,* is in preparation.

A specialist in African and Caribbean literature, he has published several plays and poetry collections, including *Poetry of Haitian Independence* (Yale), a number in Louisiana French poetry and theater, including *Creole Echoes: The Francophone Poetry of 19th-Century Louisiana;* and two plays: Victor Séjour's five-act drama *The Jew of Seville ("Diégarias")* and the five-act prose drama *The Fortune-Teller ("La Tireuse de cartes").* He has also translated several volumes of 19th-Century French farce.

TITLES FROM BLACK WIDOW PRESS
TRANSLATION SERIES

A Life of Poems, Poems of a Life by Anna de Noailles.
Translated by Norman R. Shapiro.
Introduction by Catherine Perry.

Approximate Man and Other Writings by Tristan Tzara.
Translated and edited by Mary Ann Caws.

Art Poétique by Guillevic.
Translated by Maureen Smith.

The Big Game by Benjamin Péret.
Translated with an introduction by Marilyn Kallet.

Boris Vian Invents Boris Vian: A Boris Vian Reader.
Edited and translated by Julia Older.

Capital of Pain by Paul Eluard.
Translated by Mary Ann Caws, Patricia Terry, and
Nancy Kline.

Chanson Dada: Selected Poems by Tristan Tzara. Translated
with an introduction and essay by Lee Harwood.

Earthlight (Clair de Terre) by André Breton.
Translated by Bill Zavatsky and Zack Rogow.
(New and revised edition.)

Essential Poems and Prose of Jules Laforgue.
Translated and edited by Patricia Terry.

*Essential Poems and Writings of Joyce Mansour:
A Bilingual Anthology.* Translated with an introduction by
Serge Gavronsky.

*Essential Poems and Writings of Robert Desnos:
A Bilingual Anthology.* Edited with an introduction and
essay by Mary Ann Caws.

EyeSeas (Les Ziaux) by Raymond Queneau.
Translated with an introduction by Daniela Hurezanu and
Stephen Kessler.

Fables in a Modern Key by Pierre Coran.
Translated by Norman R. Shapiro. Full-color illustrations
by Olga Pastuchiv.

Fables of Town & Country by Pierre Coran.
Translated by Norman R. Shapiro. Full-color illustrations
by Olga Pastuchiv.

Forbidden Pleasures: New Selected Poems 1924–1949
by Luis Cernuda. Translated by Stephen Kessler.

Furor and Mystery & Other Writings by René Char.
Translated by Mary Ann Caws and Nancy Kline.

*The Gentle Genius of Cécile Périn: Selected Poems (1906–
1956).* Edited and translated by Norman R. Shapiro.

Guarding the Air: Selected Poems of Gunnar Harding.
Translated and edited by Roger Greenwald.

Howls & Growls: French Poems to Bark By.
Translated by Norman R. Shapiro; illustrated by
Olga K. Pastuchiv. *(forthcoming)*

I Have Invented Nothing: Selected Poems
by Jean-Pierre Rosnay. Translated by J. Kates.

In Praise of Sleep: Selected Poems of Lucian Blaga
Translated with an Introduction by Andrei Codrescu.

The Inventor of Love & Other Writings by Gherasim Luca.
Translated by Julian & Laura Semilian. Introduction by
Andrei Codrescu. Essay by Petre Răileanu.

Jules Supervielle: Selected Prose and Poetry.
Translated by Nancy Kline & Patricia Terry.

La Fontaine's Bawdy by Jean de La Fontaine.
Translated with an introduction by Norman R. Shapiro.

Last Love Poems of Paul Eluard.
Translated with an introduction by Marilyn Kallet.

Love, Poetry (L'amour la poésie) by Paul Eluard.
Translated with an essay by Stuart Kendall.

Pierre Reverdy: Poems, Early to Late.
Translated by Mary Ann Caws and Patricia Terry.

Poems of André Breton: A Bilingual Anthology.
Translated with essays by Jean-Pierre Cauvin
and Mary Ann Caws.

Poems of A. O. Barnabooth by Valery Larbaud.
Translated by Ron Padgett and Bill Zavatsky.

Poems of Consummation by Vicente Aleixandre.
Translated by Stephen Kessler.

Préversities: A Jacques Prévert Sampler.
Translated and edited by Norman R. Shapiro.

RhymAmusings (AmuseRimes) by Pierre Coran.
Translated by Norman R. Shapiro.

The Sea and Other Poems by Guillevic.
Translated by Patricia Terry. Introduction by
Monique Chefdor.

Through Naked Branches by Tarjei Vesaas.
Translated, edited, and introduced by Roger Greenwald.

To Speak, to Tell You? Poems by Sabine Sicaud.
Translated by Norman R. Shapiro. Introduction and notes
by Odile Ayral-Clause.

MODERN POETRY SERIES

BARNSTONE, WILLIS.
ABC of Translation
African Bestiary: Poems and Drawings for All Ages
    (forthcoming)

BRINKS, DAVE.
The Caveat Onus
The Secret Brain: Selected Poems 1995–2012

CESEREANU, RUXANDRA.
Crusader Woman. Translated by Adam J. Sorkin.
    Introduction by Andrei Codrescu.
Forgiven Submarine
    by Ruxandra Cesereanu and Andrei Codrescu.

ESHLEMAN, CLAYTON.
An Alchemist with One Eye on Fire
Anticline
Archaic Design
Clayton Eshleman/The Essential Poetry: 1960–2015
Grindstone of Rapport: A Clayton Eshleman Reader
Penetralia
Pollen Aria **(forthcoming)**
The Price of Experience
Curdled Skulls: Poems of Bernard Bador. Translated by
    Bernard Bador with Clayton Eshleman.
Endure: Poems by Bei Dao.
    Translated by Clayton Eshleman and Lucas Klein.

JORIS, PIERRE.
Barzakh (Poems 2000–2012)
Exile Is My Trade: A Habib Tengour Reader

KALLET, MARILYN.
How Our Bodies Learned
The Love That Moves Me
Packing Light: New and Selected Poems
Disenchanted City (La ville désenchantée) by Chantal
    Bizzini. Translated by J. Bradford Anderson,
    Darren Jackson, and Marilyn Kallet.

KELLY, ROBERT.
Fire Exit
The Hexagon

KESSLER, STEPHEN.
Garage Elegies

LAVENDER, BILL.
Memory Wing

LEVINSON, HELLER.
from stone this running
LinguaQuake
Tenebraed
Un-
Wrack Lariat

OLSON, JOHN.
Backscatter: New and Selected Poems
Dada Budapest
Larynx Galaxy

OSUNDARE, NIYI.
City Without People: The Katrina Poems

ROBERTSON, MEBANE.
An American Unconscious
Signal from Draco: New and Selected Poems

ROTHENBERG, JEROME.
Concealments and Caprichos
Eye of Witness: A J. Rothenberg Reader.
    Edited with commentaries by Heriberto Yepez &
    Jerome Rothenberg.
The President of Desolation & Other Poems

SAÏD, AMINA.
The Present Tense of the World: Poems 2000 – 2009.
    Translated with an introduction by Marilyn Hacker.

SHIVANI, ANIS.
Soraya (Sonnets)

WARD, JERRY W., JR.
Fractal Song

ANTHOLOGIES / BIOGRAPHIES

Barbaric Vast & Wild: A Gathering of Outside and
    Subterranean Poetry (Poems for the Millennium,
    vol. 5). Editors: Jerome Rothenberg and John
    Bloomberg-Rissman

Clayton Eshleman: The Whole Art by Stuart Kendall

Revolution of the Mind: The Life of André Breton
    by Mark Polizzotti